She Needed Mirrors

by
City Taylor

COPYWRIGHT

ISBN: 979-8-9958993-0-3

Cover Photograph: Owen Lang

Published: June 9th, 2026.

Editing, Formatting, Style: Myself

website: citytaylor.org

AKNOWLEDGMENTS

my family that loves me endlessly

my many soulmates

the intelligence of the universe
always guiding me
even when I'm not looking

TABLE OF CONTENTS

There are three versions of you:

The way that you view yourself.
The way that you view other people.
The way that you view the world.

At the time that this poetry began... I recieved a strange message.

"it most certainly is. At the end of the day, a painting is simply an
unspoken expression of pure beauty, which you certainly embody,
So think of yourself as a painting, as a statue, as a beautiful
mountain and as an illuminating sunrise. Because you quite literal-
ly are all those things, and more."

It surprised me, because...
I couldn't imagine why anyone would say something that
beautiful about me.

Preface:
I don't know how to feel wanted.

INTRODUCTION

There are so many things
I build all from chips
of broken glass
I found dug into sand.
"I feel like I'm on the beach",
The sun opened
my awareness
with flare.
Solar apparition.
Cosmic.
The Granules
of rocks
soft and pillowy.
This beach.
These pieces of glass, never clear.
yet I feel I see it all my own way.
I-
I feel so special
It is shining green,
deep brown,
flowing blue.
Through these
glamorous pieces
of trash,
I find exactly what I want to see.
If I needed to see it clearly?
To leave this beautiful, sandy getaway...
I spin around,
speak to the horizon,
and am met with more sand.
The same waves.
They screeched all around me.
The shores open book revealing
such simple truths I fade from,
I read it as gospel.

I WANT TO TAKE SACRED OFFERINGS
OFFERINGS
OFF THE ALTAR

IWTTSOOTA

I

They swam in droves
to taste
of her flesh.
But what was left?
Harmonies of humans.
People
that crave salvation
from that of
a harlet.

IWTTSOOTA
II

You've said that I am sweet.
It's funny,
how easy it is for you to be mean to me.
Don't you like
how I'm personable?
Well,
I'm not nice.
I'm caring.
I make friends but I'm sly.
There's snakes in my closet.
I promise,
you'll regret it.
Just dare me.

IWTTSOOTA
III

5

What you gave me-
It was everything,
We weren't dating-
I needed you.
It was indecent.
I keep what I stole.
I hope that's okay
with you.
I can't forget.
I want it badly.

IWTTSOOTA
IV

A solemn young boy
No...
A young girl.
A love interest
of mine.
The one I
dreamt of many years ago...
Has disappeared.
She learned to former inner peace
with pieces
of my puzzle.
I was only inspirational to you,
 never your equal.

IWTTSOOTA
V

Do I feel like I'm free ?
He saved what he gave to me.
If I'm better now,
I wish I felt that way.
If it saves me,
I'd like it to be given please.
Hold my hands out, delicate...
or like so sudden and definite.
It takes too long.
I've said it before.
I hate waiting.
So why am I even here,
asking?

Why do these images make me think of you?
I tell you I journal about you; but why?

THE AIRPLANE RIDE

TAR
I

They're out of vodka.
I'll take a story instead.
I'm not feeling right.
If this plane doesn't crash,
I'll have gin instead.

TAR
II

I know that
I'm broken.
Not
like shattered glass.
More like
an empty lot.
Where a church
used to be.
I'm just not sure what to build instead.

TAR
III

Watching a show
I think you'd like.
I try to watch it
like you would.
If only you were here instead.

TALE OF A RUNAWAY BRIDE

TOARB
I

I cut and paste
and superglue
my problems
to the back of my skull.
Stamp my eyes shut.
This vessel I inhabit
feels only true pain inside.
This chest.
Cavity.
Where I occupy.
To escape is to be loved.
To escape you must please me.
Need me.
I need to run.

TOARB
II

It all puddles beneath me.
Empowered crimson.
All these years have just made their bed with me.
Longevity.
The bickering
snickering
memories
bundled tight
with an imbecile
stick.
Tied with ribbon.
It's impartial
that I run.
so far away
from the perception
I held so dear.
Yet,
this feminine desire is the only thing
I have left.
Best Regards,
My Fragileness.
My brokenness.
My idealism.

TOARB
III.I

I'm tired
of taking pictures
at someone else's
fucking wedding.
When do I get to wear white?
Let loose
clear plans illustrated
by my own
concussive chaos
so beautiful
because
I might've been
worth it
to be in
someone
else's
vows.
Now,
wouldn't it be nice
to stain it chocolate
with cake?
The flavors
I longed for,
adore.
Me and her don't mix.
I don't usually do that sort of stuff.

TOARB
III.II

Anyway,
I sent out invites
for a party
I wasn't invited to.
I like to stand across
from the door.
Be all red.
So,
I can be jealous.
After all,
It's okay.
I used to live there,
play there.
Not anymore.
I grab onto my wrist
smack my hand on tile
and go to work.
I wear long sleeves.
Who wants to
see me naked
anyway.

CHICKADEES
I

18

Chattering.
Many beautiful chickadees.
Sprawled atop my windowsill.
Outside, their families await.
They twiddle and chirp
around my house.
At night,
There are times
I wish I could exist
where you do.
I don't open doors.
If I tell you goodnight
they'll stop singing.

I stopped talking.

I CAN'T LOOK UP
AT THE SKY
BECAUSE THEN
I'LL KNOW
THERE'S MORE
OUT THERE
WAITING FOR ME

ICLUATSBTIKTMOTWFM
I

Stumbling
on my own two feet.
Reeling in feeble tithes.
I gather them
on a glass yard.
See below me the trees,
the evergreen
entrances me.
I glanced up,
and dropped
down
into an
emerald lake.
Blizzards rang
down the hills.
Crumpled all the oak.
As the water froze over me,
I went inside
to bring up
what I had collected throughout my life.
Realizing I had left it behind,
my hands are empty.

ICLUATSBTIKTMOTWFM
II

She rose
to see her body
across from her.
Gilded,
the sides
of the mirror.
Her eyes.
Void of attention,
Rolling in tandem,
She twirled slowly.
In the mirror
was someone
no one recognized.
Here lies a corpse.
Twirling.
With simple eyes.
Void of attention.
Rolling in tandem.
That stared back at her,
mimicking

ICLUATSBTIKTMOTWFM
III

23

When the light fades,
she is set free
into embassy.
She is a black dove,
so peaceful
when taking flight.
Manifesting.
I hold my wishes
in cold hands.
Such illusions would fluster,
all that appears
writhes in dismay.
I will stay
in the dark.

ICLUATSBTIKTMOTWFM
IV

Rays
of light
seem dim.
Every morning
I wake up
still dreaming.
Not about anyone
or anything in particular.
My world is a tv screen.
Fogs
on my windshield.
Steam
on my mirror.
Sight that
blends with
my reflection.
My hands are floating.
I can't be this anymore.

ICLUATSBTIKTMOTWFM
V

25

How I wished to believe in efficacy.
If I could be less clumsy.
Windows I jam.
Clipped wires
I've tripped on.
I take small sips of water
before I leave my bed.
I walk into my living room
to lay on the sofa.
Upon my fabulous assortment
of crystal gems,
delirium potions.
I lay about thee,
of my material possessions.
Above me,
I ponder my dwelling.
The ceiling.
Popped and dried dripping cotton,
The things I hold dearly.
Layden so loosely beside me.
I empty my glass
by full plates
I never finish.

ICLUATSBTIKTMOTWFM VI

All I See Are Lilac Skys

I went to sleep
in a world
that held no parts of me.
So, I woke up in a place
That was quite the same.
I'm always dreaming.
So,
even though my eyes stay open
and the faces that I see,
or things that involve me,
just seem
to happen around me!
I say sorry.
Keep my wits about me.
If that's the only thing
I can do.
I don't need to be here.
I'm just an unfinished book
looking upwards towards the sky.
I'm an unwound cassette tape.

ICLUATSBTIKTMOTWFM
VII

27

The sun don't shine for no one.
Oh,
I need it.
If it would,
I need it to live forever.
The other day-
I saw how big
the sky could be.
Afraid of falling,
I strap myself down.
If it really mattered
how high up I could go.
I lay close to the floor
just to feel the warmth
of the sun again.

ICLUATSBTIKTMOTWFM
VIII.I

I find myself in cold showers-
long drives-
going 85 an hour.
I see myself
in duck ponds.
Tiny shop windowpanes.
I can't close my eyes.
To be myself?
I think I'm broken.
Something about
the way I was raised.
Everything I've come to know.
I feel unsure
In my waking moments.

ICLUATSBTIKTMOTWFM
VIII.II

I'll lose myself to the idea,
The hallmarks of my own serenity.
A sweet little butterfly interrupts my thoughts.
I just need to muster up the courage,
pull myself together,
and grow into a big tree.
Then I wouldn't
have to experience anything.
I'd be wood.
Wood would be me.

ICLUATSBTIKTMOTWFM
IX

I look up to find
a stout angel atop my ear,
drumming up the courage to speak to me.
I'll start with an interjection.
That:
"It's not fair!"
"You're bothering me!"
I see it shocked,
red in the face.
Looking away.
I frown.
I'm not ready to hear
what you have to say.
I'm keen on
my own disposition.
I know it's frivolous.
My hearts just beating too fast.
I'd like to be left alone.
I bide my time.
Dying on hills
I shouldn't have climbed.

ICLUATSBTIKTMOTWFM
X

Sometimes I write things down
just to cross them out.
Called my friend grace
just so I could hang up the phone.
Ordered a cup of coffee
just to walk out the door.
Turning my car on
just to walk back inside.
Cutting up fruit
just toss it in the garbage.
I lay down.
I close my eyes.

ICLUATSBTIKTMOTWFM
XI.I

Beautiful.
I can see myself hanging.
Out of the corner of my eye
I can see it.
What a marvel I could be,
just that much closer.
Stop clinging to life Hannah.
I wish
I were more limp
instead of writhing.
You must be entirely too frail.
Soft to the touch.
So that you may meet your creed
headfirst.
Such an ancient deceit
to off myself
alone
above tile floor.
I do not need
a concrete reason
to continue going-
I am allergic to living.
Splinters of all composite nightmares are apparent now.
My eyes began to hollow years ago.

ICLUATSBTIKTMOTWFM
XI.II

33

I'm just a stupid puppy with parvo.
They put those down all the time.
Why isn't my wave still waning?
Enchanting ribbons of pressure
surround me.
I tie the loose ends behind my neck.
Impossible to wonder,
What could I have done differently?
I'm the problem.
They all ask questions unanswered.
I'd leave no note
and no one would find me
for days.

ICLUATSBTIKTMOTWFM
XII

34

I smelled it again today.
You blink.
There it is again.
Oh my god oh gentle
ebb n flow the flutter
of small wings.
Soft echoes and singing.

ICLUATSBTIKTMOTWFM
XIII

It feels so cold.
Yet,
there's the sun.
Taunting me.
It feels like
it just snowed
yesterday.
The bruises never go away.
Let me ask insead.
The bruises never go away,
do they?

ICLUATSBTIKTMOTWFM
XIV

36

When I die
it will be quiet.
I'll stop believing in magic
and fairies
too.
I'll stop talking.
My earth will dry up.
I'll stop watering my oceans.
Then,
I'll put out my last candle.
My room will be brown.
The carpet will be red.
Maybe I just need
to disappear for a while.
Be myself a little longer.
I let go of being perfect
a long time ago.
It still hurts.

ICLUATSBTIKTMOTWFM
XV

37

In an attempt to placate
my imminent desire,
I've lifted my eyes
from the ground
to face
the abundant things
I've come to cherish.
I am caught
between
the guise of my heart;
Which is mewing.
Frail like a newborn.
My mind
that sputters and whirls
like an old clock that needs oiling.
My lack of convergence
became juxtaposed
to the blank slate of
notebook paper
I've criss crossed
with black marker.

CHICKADEES
II

There're those damn birds.
That stand tall
Behind curtains.
They sing and
it's loud.
It hurts.
They're screaming at me.
Leading me.
If only
I wanted to hurt them.
Make them shut up.
They'd stop singing.

It's easy if no one
want's to see you naked...
right?

I DON'T WANNA BE A CLEANING LADY

IDWBACL
I

I'd rather it be over.
Than just fine.
I love cooking.
I just don't know how to clean.
No one taught me
to clean while you cook.
But I promise...
The food will still be good.
I made it just for you.

IDWBACL
II.I

I miss drawing circles
with my friends.
Candles all around us.
I miss when we sat on roofs,
wearing old sweaters
and flannel.
The crisp winter caresses my cheek,
carrying the wind of sacred memory.
I realize how I drown
myself in character.

IDWBACL
II.II

43

I wanted
everything we went through
to mean something.
Now I see
the world is changing.
Something old
Something new
Something borrowed
Something blue.
Visions of renaissance.
A
Fucking redemption arc.
I wanted
To
Usher in
A
Furtherment of change.
Without saying what I mean.

IDWBACL
III

I left a small town.
The memories blacked out.
Back then?
It was all I knew.
Not long ago,
no one ever sang my name.
So many wishes,
the hopes we dreamed,
So long ago.
I haven't forgotten.
Not a single word.
Amongst my column pillared prison,
I am just remembering
such apparent dislike
of my architecture.
I'm not a building.
I don't feel your presence
if you're not around.

IDWBACL
IV

45

Oops.
There we go again.
I let it slip.
Crack.
A fierce whip,
Not my own.
It snaps out from within me.
New Arms!
Sprouting where my head should be.
It's so like me, but I just don't need it.
These whips have spikes,
with flowers
coming off the end.
I let them rest in my hair by my eyes.
Just when you go to reach for them:
'It's coming." I say.
Whether you like it or not.

IDWBACL
V

46

Brown walls.
Lack stains.
Bred dirty tidy.
Licked the downward.
Scents rub peculiar holes
down into a rubble dam.

IDWBACL
VI

She ran in circles til her feet were raw.
Just to
Stamp
her mouth
on
welcome mats.
Lick moldy floors.
Unclean
is the stickiness
between her fingers.
She rubbed her eyes red
with stained cheeks,
pursed lips.

IDWBACL
VII

48

I lay down.
Just when I wake,
I feel it waning.
I know it'll disappear.
I look anyway.
This transparent town.
I can see right through it.
I'm sick of feeling clean.

IDWBACL
VIII

My job
Is to feel clean
and pretty.
I wouldn't go to work
if I didn't feel inclined

Key Word:
Insecurity.

SHE NEEDED MIRRORS

SNM
I.I

Hand me greased,
golden,
scissors.
So, I may
cut the string
that bound my eyes
to screens.
The only thread
that ever held me down
was standing still.
My feet.
that stood
firm
on bleached wool.

SNM
I.II

53

I'm tired of mirrors
I never want to see
People on screens
stare back at me.
I surround myself with mirrors
cameras all around me.
I change my face
every day.
It's still the same.
I'm so tired of
never feeling
anything,
All I do
is change my face
my hair
my body.
Every day.
It's still the same.
I change my face my hair and my body.
It's still the same
It will always be that way.

SNM
II

54

Shards slither out
from caves of beauty,
Reflection, opaque, unseeing.
Standpoints,
opposite to knowing,
Shining becomes
a synonym
for demons.
At the pinnacle,
resurface from emptiness.

SNM
III

55

Pass it to me.
I say it
all the time.
I've just learnt
it's better
when
I don't mean it.
I'm honest at times.
I just don't understand
whether
my window
is a mirror.
I shut my blinds this time.

SNM
IV

Swollen.
My
hands
filled
with
malice.
Tearing at my eyes.
I don't want to look at myself anymore.
I'll free myself
of
this image that
I never
wanted to see.

SNM
V

It's impossible.
I'm intrigued.
I've always wondered
about my relationship
with strangers
I smile at
across
the street.
Then.
I remember,
How I sat there.
Staring at those deer,
listening to the frogs sing.

SNM
VI

Detached from solemn eyes,
a genius watches a film.
Sequestered in a white chair.
In an empty room
to match.
The walls ooze black muck.
It came up to her knees.
She would wade around the room,
so upset of the floor.
Shedding tear after tear.
Then,
a door appeared.
Crimson,
Or
Brick.
Standard size.
Never locked.
She would pass over the knob;
Yet her eyes...
They worked fine.
It had yet to seem the option for her.

SNM
VII

59

I'm healing.
I'm stuck with this heart
that won't stop beating.
Scabs
that stop me
from leaving
The house.
Yet,
my newfound
agoraphobia
unleashes worlds
inside my brain.
Leading me inwards.
Escaping a world
I wished
I could know.

SNM
VIII.I

60

Am I pretty to you?
I meet people.
They love me.
Just once.
They look into my eyes.
I let them touch me.
Is my skin soft?
Tender for you?
I live in mirrors
left behind.
Melted,
the ice sculptures
on display.

SNM
VIII.II

Does it matter where it's been?
Will I ever be more than just an exhibit
to you?
What keeps me sane at night
is that.
I only exist in fleeting moments.
Surface level.
Then nothing.

SNM

IX

I stay warm.
I wish
I was comfortable
and kind
like you.
You stay
cool
and comfortable
when you sit in a room.
I wonder what you think about.

SNM
X

I'm a cat.
You love dogs.
We just don't get along.
I've been dreaming
all about you
every night too.
I wake up sweating.
Let's just face
The fact that I'm crazy.
Nobody wants to be around me.
I hate myself this way.
It's just all the time.

SNM
XI

64

I see you.
The way you work with power tools.
Addicted to being haunted.
I wonder if I'm that way.
When I act like you:
Ohhh,
How many good things
I've destroyed.

SNM
XII

They knew I was different
when I would get a cut
and it never healed.
Once,
we shared
a nick
on our nose.
We looked the same.
Mine stayed, while
Yours just faded away.
They knew I was different
when I would tell them a story,
and we would repeat its contents.
I knew this, too.
They knew I was different:
When I kept my word,
while they kept theirs
hidden from me.
I knew I was different
because I can't quite learn my lesson,
and you can't wrap that in bandages.

SNM
XIII

66

Something ended.

I've cried it all away.

Now I'm a girl

holding broken glass

that's craving for skin.

Dicohtomy.
I'm tired of finding
all the shit
I never look for.

INTAGIBLE (VISIONS)
FEAR (+ ILLUSION)

I(V)F(+I)
I

Deep imbedded
in the harsh quality of light.
Unknown Babylon.
There is no singular reality.
I just see things.
Molding concepts.
I cannot be here anymore.
Silently fretting.
I sit calmly.
It sets in.

I(V)F(+I)
II

Tapping on the window.
A smile so breathy.
That smacks its lips.
It's gaze seeking.
So excited to meet me!
Behind a locked glass pane.
Turquoise beads
stare back at me.
Waiting.

I(V)F(+I)
III

Answered below
symphonic telephones.
Hearts unheard of.
Screeching kings
layer orders.
Sunk into peasants,
Skin tears and
Resigns.
Blackens without forgiveness.
Unkind sutures
associated with light
that get left behind.

I(V)F(+I)
IV

Wars start after beady eyes.
At bludgeoning street.
You haven't been, obviously.
It's at the back of her skull.
Knocking the wind in.
THIS HURTS!!!!!
She screams
to an assailant.
The one that
cracked her head out.
The reverberation
hums within her.
Ringing through her toes
to the tip of her nose.

I(V)F(+I)
V

Smash.
I hear of a comet
hurdling towards earth.
It whisps, soars.
Cracking its whip at me.
It whispers my name in its
descent.
I lay flat against the ground.
Shuddering.
My teeth are chattering.
That tremor
on impact
vibrates through me.
juhIf I were glass,
I'dve shattered.
But,
I'm flesh.
So,
I splat.

I(V)F(+I)
VI.I

I used to be scared
of finding needles in the public chairs.
Theatres,
Auditoriums,
Classrooms.
Razorblades on waterslides.
Put there precisely for me.
Maybe it wouldn't hurt?
Or maybe
It'd have
someone's blood
on it?
Slice me open;
I'd get sick.
I'd go to the hospital.
I'd have no life anymore.
I'd be so ill.
Pricked by foreign metal.

I(V)F(+I)
VI.II

I found a needle
in the seat in front of me.
It didn't prick me.
It just stared at me.
I know that...
If I wanted to touch it,
I could.
I'll leave it there, instead.
It won't prick anyone.
It's not under me.
Right in front.
Where I can see.

CHICKADEES
III

76

I found myself
genuinely believing
in the
charming
chickadee
soliloquies.
Nurturing my own disposition,
I'm securing
disappointment
in my gaze.
I watch myself
in the condensed windows.
Holding onto my annoyance
is exhausting,
It manifests as a low hanging cloud around me.
This fog is neutral
and never ending.

DEEP DOWN
I LIKE WHO I AM

dark eyes
pure
ascension
divine

They're mine.

empty
baskets
woven
with
interstellar colors
that rippled
all
brown

"Let me be sexy!"
"I need to be hot to have meaning!"
-        **Prayed** the lonely girl.

HOW TO GROW YOUR
VERY OWN
ROSE GARDEN

HTGYVORG
I

Ode to A Poison Flower

Your sniff
is so serving.
Oh' mankai,
Oh' illustrious.
My nature.
The tingle
up my nose.
Throughout me.
My heart stops
and starts for you.
So succubus
in writing.
It makes me think.
Divine,
like chaos.
Unnerving.
To be mine.
To be one.
Like you.

HTGYVORG
II

SYMPHONY!

Alive.
It was sweet.
Crunching leaves.
They gave it to
just you.
A secret.
A rune.
auja
Let it flow through you.
Jealous vines
consumed you.

HTGYVORG
III

I'm tired of being responsible
for that hags old garden.
I moved into her worn out house,
and thought I'd be safe here.
Yet,
her garden still grows.
She's long gone?
Or so I thought…
I tried to dry it out.
I'm allergic to lilies
and roses.
They come every year.
Suffocating me
with the aroma.
Humans on chessboards
laugh at me.
How I crave
perfection
to falsify
my own games.
Black and white.
Good and evil.
The master of the board
Is more than one color.

HTGYVORG
IV

Sensory, calmness.
Silken sheets.
delicately cascade.
Laden on hills
of dirt.
Hidden over burnt grains.
Old memories.
Blooms form
from corpses
of my past.
People who took
seeds
from my garden
for theirs.
Blood sacks
pop
to fill
the dirt with
nutrients.
Pain fell into growth patterns
that resembles itself.

HTGYVORG
V

84

It was fire.
Compensation?
She lacked.
What she lacked in compassion,
turned futures behind them.
I laid beside you
to become roots.
It'd love to suck it all away.
The good parts.
Until there was nothing.

HTGYVORG
VI

85

I move the rocks around my garden
laid so ornate and tidy.
I count.
Up and down.
I lay myself neatly between them.
The supple sun supplies my desperate desires.
It lets loose this inner fire all my own.
I noticed it's been quiet.
So,
I scream.
"I'M SO JEALOUS!"
I sit up
to place myself
so sweetly next to a sandstone
I bash my head into it.

HTGYVORG
VII

I need to do something right.
I'm plainly gathering seeds
fallen aside of a lemon tree.
I am immune to the nitrogen
that is necessary
to foster growth.
I know that I must cross a raveen
that I so consciously
decided to leave behind.
Liken yourself
to the crows pecking at
rotten fruit
that fell off the tree.
Don't tell newton please.
I remember the saying,
I just stopped caring.
When life hands you a lemon,
You just have to accept that
instead of making lemonade,
you must grow a whole new lemon tree.
All on your own.

HTGYVORG
VIII.I

No longer free to roam,
I've succumbed to my alabaster skin.
Fashioning rubies
where my nails should be.
I scratch at a nearby fence.
I saw their garden.
I grew envious.
Posted against my own patience,
I swallow it down
until it blisters my neck raw.
My willingness for solitude caught up to me.
Shouting itself and bearing my name.
It's indisposed to my home.

HTGYVORG
VIII.II

Unannounced
was a pestilence born
from my
yesterdays.
Feasting itself until
it became a creature
of its own.
I gawked.
I just stood there
as it seeped into
the tile floor.
Leaking outwards
throughout the lawn.
I lost it when I found my rose dead.
I'm not prepared to face this Tulpa.
I willow myself now,
haphazardly swaying in the wind.
I wish I were a real tree.
For now,
I continue believing.
Clawing for dreams that were never
mine to keep.

HTGYVORG
XI

Unequivocal rhymes.
There are many things to see.
I see nothing.
I feel though.
They are thrush,
lively vegetation,
from inside.
Sprouts catering
to
my fragile demeanor.
Demented are
the creatures I taste.
Pleasantry.
I spin elegantly.
I take the first step,
following destiny.
I'm a lot of things.
Owned?
Is not one of them.

CHICKADEES
IV

90

What lonely angles
sprung up
to create.
Lovingly.
Writing Concerto's
about Things.
Like clockwork,
they sing.
Tiny,
friendly,
chickadees.
Strung out about thee.
There was nothing I missed about having these.

It sopped wet with water.
Did you mean to ruin it?
Is it true?
You never had anything to say to me.
Did you?

WHAT HAPPENS WHEN
A SIREN
DOESN'T SING?

WHWASDS?

I

I was born
in a rainstorm.
Screaming terribly.
Every time
someone dies,
I can feel tiny drops, and
grey clouds all about.
I wonder,
when it rains...
If It'll be my turn.

WHWASDS?
II

It's not fair
that I'm allergic to energy.
I try to breathe in,
and exhale.
There she goes.
I start exploding.
I lose my grip, and..
There!
It's looming.
The Depth,
Deep,
Wine,
Waters.
Begging, their whispers call.
Drawing me in.
Sirens pale in aptitude
to the lake.
I'll just take one dip.
Let me put my head under.
I'll be fine.

WHWASDS?
III

I let go of my illusive rain.
Then,
it takes hold,
and becomes me.
I just needed a break from it all.
I sink knee deep into the water while walking.
So gentle
the lake
the waves are waning.
I don't believe in the moon.
She laughs and just taunts me.
"We were born on the same day."
She said.
I ignore her.
She's always there.
Waiting.
I bleach my whites,
only to resurrect them
with red dye.

WHWASDS?
IV

96

The times I cried
alone on the street.
The things I missed.
Those cherished things
I thought I loved.
They vanished.
I let it fall/flow around me.
What sweet miracles disburse
throughout me.

WHWASDS?
V

But all I ever wanted was that.
I don't indulge.
Despair on requiems.
Diaspora in veiled acronyms.
Bellied in depths of coal.
Ripples made by me.
Dropping piece by piece,
all boar in sacks
tugged shut.

WHWASDS?
VI

98

I have these dreams
that I wake up from.
I do it then.
Cold showers.
I gasp under it.
Cool,
clear, white walls.

WHWASDS?
VII

You seek justice from an apostle without conviction.
There's nothing left to take.
I seek something bigger.
I've waited
just for this moment.
I broke my heart already so long ago,
and gave myself away.
My lovely body.
I gave it away to Jesus.
He switched silently,
handing me down to earth again.
Catatonic.
I lay there untouched on old soil,
just waiting for it to rain.

WHWASDS?
VIII

I'm afraid that it won't be a miracle.
If I could be so so excited?
Ready?
Like my rain it must be so common,
right?
Just fear.
Unsure of what likely lays ahead.
Our world is torn between fate and destiny.
The people that waste away in soil.
Fermented alcohol.
Dead dandelions.

WHWASDS?
IX

I take it slow.
Why does it always
end so fast?
I'm neck deep
in water.
I always knew
I was a river
bound for an exit.
I was never ready.
I'm neck deep in water.
Not ready to drown.
He could not bear
the sight of me.
I could not bear
to stare.
I sank into it.
Believing that you
were all I needed to breathe.

WHWASDS?
X

I descend from high rocks,
pushing my bare feet into firm sand.
I jumped off these same rocks as a child.
My ankle is creaking in palpable memory.
It helped many times
to urge my mind back to reality.
Much like returning tides,
There's this little thing I do.
My ankle always cracks when I shift it in circles.
Oh, how
many
times
have I spun my foot around
to sense it.
It
leads me back to the cool waves.
The salty wind.
Such a strange feeling.
Much to my dismay...
I can't stop myself.
The pondering of what the beach might feel like
once I leave again.

WHWASDS?
XI

Curiosity.
Painful is a lust for knowledge.
To hold any truth to be self-evident
makes me feel ill.
Used to be,
my life would change under storms.
Now it is rains,
and nothing seems to change.
Quivering,
the droplets fell down my cheeks
where my tears should be.
Curiosity killed the cat.
So,
I became a mouse instead.
Rummaging through trash
in search of meaning.
In search of
where someone's treasure might be.

WHWASDS?
XII

I was not born in a rainstorm.
I must've misheard
sorrow for sympathy.
Much like flowers I assume are pink,
are just closer to red,
maybe orange.
I take small steps out of my perception,
to find depth alone.
I find myself bracing
for the sky to fall inwards,
for a secret to come exploding out of nothing.
A long-awaited comet
that rushes down onto me.
I let go of my interpretation,
to play the hands I'm dealt.
Just let the sun shine.
If it rains,
I'll let it wash over me.
As if it meant nothing.

CHERRIES

C

I

List me in your favorite tastes.
I bear bountiful fruit for your basket.
Let me end up in the pits of your stomach where I'll rot.

C
II

I had this dream that I woke up from.
It was kissing you.
Lavish pillows we loved on.
Flowers that grew where we lay.
I fell deep into my longing.
For those felt parts of you.
I lay in my waking.
For a while,
I keep thinking.
'I won't sleep the same.'

C
III

Placed in adequate normalcy:
Cosmic, surreal.
"Follow me."
No one led we.
Tweed, fennel.
Concealed.
Wrapping love.
I melt in colors
just to experience
red wine found in abandoned cupboards.
Human mind.
It is free.
Like honey.
Sweet and savory.
Money.
Bite size.
She sleeps.

C
IV

Each step
is that
same waning.
Pestilence is an un-held hand.
I am utterly drawn to yearning.
I let it start at my toes-
Creeping all the way up
to the top of my head.
Spilling upwards towards
the Aether...
I love this feeling.
It frees me from old chains
that wore down my shoulders.
I'm the crooked neck girl.
It is the strongest perspective.
God, This world.
I hope too,
that if someone yearned for me,
wishing on the stars, the moon-
they've never talked to.
"I want to be next to you."
Spoken on cue.
Maybe we feel the same way?

C
V

Share a smoke or a bite?
It means more to me
than something quiet.
I'm a bit impervious
to rational.
I wish it was more
than one moment.
You've left me here.
wondering how you'd feel,
when it's gone.

C
VI

I beg to God about you.
I beg that he keeps your hair
the same color
As you grow.
I'd be there,
Even if it's wrong.
If somehow, someway,
your hair turned grey
instead of strawberry.
It wouldn't matter.
I'm rather fond of the way it sits.
I love your good hair day.
I remember it
specifically.
I.
And that smile!
It reminds me of
Orange
And powder
And pine.

C
VII.I

Every evening
I roam in gardens I don't belong.
I long forbidden fruit
I have no taste for.
I take bitter bites of plums
Undesired peaches
I have no taste for.
So much like fruit,
I am plentiful.
I was a cherry
From some tree.
You picked me,
you told me I was sweet.
So unlike me,
We shared secrets
and
interlocked legs
on the concrete.

C
VII.II

I noticed,
unlike you.
The true
Tart
Flavor
Of cherries
though.
You began to forget me.
I walk away in my longing
to find some other garden.
The truth is:
I should've been in an orchard
instead.

I'M TIRED OF PRETENDING THERE'S NOT SOMETHING BIGGER INSIDE ME

ITOPTNSBIM

I

It has come to this.
Delicate lace.
Permeated Resin.
It melts. I hold my hand out.
I seek to investigate,
finding it empty.
So barren.
If I could assimilate
to not be.
(Yet…) I am alien.
Hollow sound resonates all within me.
It spikes while I scream.
Crawling out of me.
It never noticed how it needed me.
I take in a long breathe.
One.
To remind myself.
I'm not so special.
I am plain.
It gets quieter.
"Do you remember me?"
I do.
I steep a long tea.
Hold the cream.

ITOPTNSBIM
II.I

Gauntly it welcomes me.
Electric.
It bounces inside of me.
I've been banging on my chest.
Begging to let it out.
This. Is. Energy.
I can't breathe
or see.
It's all within me.
Am I nervous?
It feels like
they all can see me.
Afraid.
The things we all see.
I heard tapping. Only me.

ITOPTNSBIM
II.II

Dance, flight
It's activated.
What elusive responsibility
I kindly lay about me.
Thumping.
All day.
It's night
Ringing.
My chest aches.
I exhaled
caught rays
of light;
Not now.
It's dark or something.
Or is it just me?
Many things
I don't believe.
That smile that beckons me.
Scratches the glass beside of me.
It's all day.
They follow me.

ITOPTNSBIM
III

Clocks scream at me,
          I lay as stone.
Having yet to experience...
            The waiting..
               It is too much.
I fail to stay in
        One moment.
Yet, there are many...
         They follow me...
            Ringing...

ITOPTNSBIM
IV

Why is it fine,
That no one can take me seriously?
I just make them laugh.
When I sing,
I can make you cry too.
I love change.
Just wait and see.

ITOPTNSBIM

V

I'm stuck in a box.
I squirm.
I want to move.
I lay in bed.
My hands and feet are hammers.
My eyes are laser beams.
I live in a dungeon.
This transparent town?
I can see right through it.
I'm sick of feeling clean.
I seek crumbled dirt.
Sullen earth.
Seep through my body
and drain my heart of
its energy.

ITOPTNSBIM
VI

Filling up essential vibrations,
I'm looking to
replace my disparity.
I find…
time to dance again!
Yet,
I'm fresh empty on melody.
It's incredible
the lengths one can go
to avoid living.
I'm Brutus to clarity,
Envious of white walls.
I'm perpetually
forcing up against them.
Elegantly forming wings with my hands.
I'm just a wasp,
wishing it were a moth.

ITOPTNSBIM
VII

This. Is. Energy.
It cultivates from the sun-
Projecting from people. .
They encase it in a daily vitamin.
Wipe it on their faces.
I scrub my face raw every single night now too.
I lick the spoon.
Inhaling aromas around me,
I lick the spoon.
Whether I am allowed to or not,
I lick the spoon.
I'm ripping up ribbons and tying up the guards of the museum.
I learn so much.
I live in the exhibits.
I mop up floods in Texas.
It rains every single day.
I sweep sand in the deserts,
I water my oceans,
to grow myself.
Clean what's normal.
Fix what is next.
I control it.

CHICKADEES
V

123

What would make me full again?
How am I whole?
Chatty little chickadees
strung about in threes.
Maybe.
<u>Just</u> maybe,
We can all sing in key.
I think they like to be around me.

THE MARRIAGE OF
PERSEPHONE
AND
DIONYSUS

TMOPAD

I

Twas a lady.
She appeared to me.
"IT IS I,
PERSEPHONE!!"
Juice seeped red my jaw
Crunched tightly.
It was my seal.
Trapped down here.
She is white silk
and wicked.
A vindictive quiet.
I heard that she knows everything.
Everybody.
I wonder
if she is everywhere.
Her eyes were dark, their
depth drew in.
Incessant portals.
She's so great.
She told me a secret.
"You are a willow tree."

TMOPAD
II

Crazy guy?
How many times
must I meet you?
Crazy guy.
Oracle.
Oh,
Begging thee to free me.
What are my stakes if I look into the mirror?
That's all I ever needed.
Dionysus.
Do I wallow in pinot rivers?
I etch into the eyes who enable me see,
dig them out with
and
LICK THE SPOON.
No matter the way
I blind that harpy.
Or
my plentiful escapades at dusk...
It seems that I just fail.
All the time.
Again:
As long as no one forgets...
I won't cease to be.
This displeases me.
I'm real.
Uneasy.

TMOPAD
III

I always thought it was me!
If I was beautiful?
Me?
Handed down,
saved.
At precisely the right time.
Perfected cue.

Mine.

It appeared to me.
Sunbeams trailing out of my curtains.
I always thought it was mystical.
Time to start approaching the window.
O,
sweet.
O,
potent.
O,
Persephone…
If I ask one thing?
How do I grow this willow tree?

TMOPAD
IV

A leopard scrambles through the jungle.
Stomping ground as the damp earth .
deafening.
Maggots fall from the leaves
onto my feet/
I squish my toes into them.
I sink into their crushed crescents.
This leopard stops still in it's tracks.
It stands straight up,
the hairs of its back
Sharpening.
I pressed my feet firmly, sticking within
the muck of their corpses.
Cocooned by their fortitude.
I reside in the end.
I muster all of my courage.
Eye to eye with the apex predator -
I realize how,
I've been living in my own creation.
This leopard is my match.
How I encounter bravery
by the escapades
of tiny little demons.

TMOPAD
V

Where is Persephone…?
Who knew I could grow?
So high.
Into a grand tree.
I was never different.
The last thing she said to me:
"Bloom every day."
I miss her.
Persephone loves pomegranate seeds.
She feasted on them in hell.
You know the story.
Generating a false ideal.
It wasn't until Persephone tasted a grape,
Gift of Dionysus.
Then,
she knew that she would ferment them with him.
Because grapes taught her something
about it.
She learned that when people leave…
Live with them.
They never die.

PINK AND BLUE
MAKE
PURPLE

PABMP

I

Blessed be for being blue.
For all the things it gave to you.
Blowing winds I see –
The freeing purple that hypnotizes me.
Winding along barren tracks...
Where we met.
We shared something.
The same journey.
The one that led you to blue -
Led me back to pink, too.

PABMP
II

Stay.
Sway with me to the melody!
I'd dance with you every day
until I die.

PABMP

III

She knew.
He knew.
Unbeknownst to one another.
They wrote stories in their heads
of something fragile.
Dependent on frivolous dreams.
It went as such:
The lion roared.
The goat crawled up mountains.
They never met.
Their paths wouldn't cross.
Yet,
the goat heard booming roars,
Yet,
the lion always viewed the mountain.
Unbeknownst to one another.
Would they ever cross senses?
Unrequited was their need for answers.
They craved.
Their imaginations flurried
An expression they did heed.
In the real world,
outside of their stories:
The Goat would be food.
The Lion would be full.
He knew he would never have enough.
She knew she wouldn't last forever.

PABMP
IV

Pisces, Neptune.
Blackberries married by Athena.
It tasted sweet.
I slept in canopies.
Dreaming soft silt,
canopied empty in sultry.
Nude beiged my darling.
Nails crested.
Nestled by
my illusive rain.
Tap tap tap
the sparkle of
Godspell
tuned the grass.

PABMP
V

A prism semblanced me.
Ricocheted around the room.
The walls vibrate,
pulsing with you.
The essence of the light.
simple,
as it enveloped me.
Life was made that day.
In the night,
we felt backed by a legacy.
Where children before me
reset a world and let it be.

PABMP
VI

Needed to fuck you so bad,
I started manifesting multiple powers.
"I pulled it."
"What?"
You know.
"The string of fate!"
I danced with it.
I learned about infinity.
It's found within a day.
Perpetual,
Like we are.
A cycle never ending.
I won't chase you.
I'm no hunter.
I just lay flat on the pavement
while clutching my stomach.
Begging for a taste.

PABMP
VII

I think you might be an angel.
But,
I know.
Deep down…
I wish I was God.
I could own the very notion of you.
Bid you to my willing.
I wish you were Jesus so you would die for me.
I would be left waiting
for you to return.

PABMP
VIII

138

There's chemistry being done.
Sensations crafted.
Our bodies textures
made for
one another.

PABMP
IX

I figured I'd stop being electric.
Bouncing from one dark corner to another.
I've been singing more.
It's all weird now.
I notice the way it follows me.
Not that my hair is frizzy.
I shock others to the touch.
I notice people more often.
In particular,
Let's just say I found the fringes of that electricity
dancing out of someone's hair.
I'd like to run my hands through it.
Instead of remembering how good it feels to be something,
to someone.
I would become that person for myself.
If I could.
I can.

It's all just a contest.

VENUS IS ALSO THE GODDESS OF VICTORY

VIATGOV

I

I took my bow at the beginning of the show.
Getting low to my knees.
Begging for roses
to prick me.
When the curtain rises,
Here I am!
On the cold stage.
The illusory audience applauds me.
Rising up,
lustrous curtains frame me.

VIATGOV
II

I wanna win.
I'd leap bounds
so I could
go home
with a trophy
and
place it on my mantel.

VIATGOV
III

I can count on
all sorts of hands
every single time
I've smiled
because something I got scared of
made me feel joy instead.
I'm a card player.
I mix with the odds.
Put me in poker,
cuz I'll smirk nonstop.
You'll never know
the misfortune
I misread.

VIATGOV
IV

I walk proudly with scars.
I am a woman from mars,
after all.
Hardened so by battle.
I walk proudly with scars.
Remnant open wounds,
never ending.
Mending my own skin.
I walk proudly with scars.
Some of them I regret
and some of them I cherish.
I walk proudly with both meaning.
Wherever they lay,
they will always look the same.
No matter their name.

VIATGOV
V

I guess I'm like a little butterfly.
Marveling at its worn cocoon.
I don't think my wings are that different.
I have an albino heart
stained red from all that blood inside.
Red can flow out of my fingers.
Run down my tear ducts.
I like bleeding.
Everyone does it.
I find now
I can show people my heart
through association.
Not everyone needs to see that it's white.
Even IF I let go
of all the red inside.
I thought I had something to prove.
But?
My wings are all I have.
With all this showing off
I can just let it go.
Feel the rain again.
I can let my flight speak for
itself.
Now,
When I think of letting myself run red:
I find that it's not so necessary.

VIATGOV
VI

You can go anywhere.
or nowhere at all.
Staying inside,
or far away places.
It's peculiar, to experience wonder,
right on your doorstep.
All one person can do, is believe.
You can. It's all within your grasp.
You don't have to do what others have dreamed of.
What is it that shines your light?
You can write your own story.
Whether you fall on hard times,
or have risen to new heights;
Write Your Story.
You could fall in love.
Break your heart to smithereens.
Write Your Story.
You could travel by bus, car, train, plane.
I walk.
Write Your Story.
It can be done anywhere,
at anytime.
Your story could be about anything.
You could be a pirate in an office chair.
A unicorn who looks outwards towards the sea.
You could just be a school teacher, a holder of knowledge,
desperately trying to give it to others.
Just write your story.
No one else can,
but you.

VIATGOV
VII

Risen afoot.
Foretelling spiral.
I sling myself upwards.
The way it spins.
I reminisce of the childhood me.
Saturn's rings ever spinning.
Intoxicating dizziness…
I was catapulted through everything.
Yet again.
Wavelength.
My ears are still ringing.
I see myself now.
Singing.

VIATGOV
VIII

It's finally happening the way that it should.
I hold my guilt
heavy
in my open palms.
My slit wrists.
Scars that are
shy of shallow.
I may hold it up
to display it proudly
for all to see.

VIATGOV
IX

Love.
It doesn't look like anything.
It just is.
Admiration.
Manifestation.
Lock it in boxes.
Keep it on display.
It is effervescent trophies
with no name.

VIATGOV
X

151

I welcome abundance.
About my face –
Inevitability is happiness
I hold for myself.
Intangible is the real, raw
scrubbing I endured.
I.
Am.
Whole.
There is no rhyme or reason.
The earth has begun chanting my name.
It is silence.
It is the wind rustling the leaves.
A kitten that entranced me.
I do not walk away from music.
I will go towards the flame – Awe inspiring.
I will not die this time.
I never needed to change.
I just love doing it.
If someone made a wish to me?
I would just grant it.
Who cares.

RIGHT BEFORE IT'S OVER
YOU GOTTA REVISIT IT
ONE LAST TIME

Every night I retreat to the bird cage
ornately hung within my home.
An old metal kennel stood tall.
Calm, crammed, hidden.
I have a long tarp over it.
I turn all the lights off and creep inside,
locking it behind me.
This is agony.
This quiet is torture.
If I am born of the feather,
Why is there metal between me,
and the song I was born to sing?

CHICKADEES DENEUMENT

The morning stays the same.
I feel so much calmer.
Little sweet birds.
Humming every morning.
They write no hymns.
Unpossesing the language I beg to keep,
unheard these messages I waited for.
Purposefully,
Methodically,
The sky just smiles upon me.
What waxing and waning appears…
I place so tenderly these
lit candles atop my windowsill.
If I know that it is wet.
Lesser,
it's dry.
Who or what I used to be.
If I could be one way,
I'd be calmly true
But what then?
I wouldn't have anything else to do.
So softly I pray about and
listen to the gentle taps on my roof.
I have these dreams that I wake up from.
I do it then.
There's so much more to do.
Even if those chickadees come back -
I tell them like it is:
"You're coming with me.
Kicking and screaming."

AT THE SUMMIT
OF ONE MOUNTAIN IS
THE BASE
OF ANOTHER

EPILOGUE
I

I emerge from
a small canopy
of fruit bearing trees.
The ancient harvest behind my exit
is fully sonder
in my hands.
I anoint them with oil,
pushing aside my strands of hair
to finally see.
It's been so long.
This knowingness grew shrubbery
around my frame.
Recently releasing me from its harness.
Knowing nothing but what the fruit taught me,
I sought out something sweet.

EPILOGUE
II

With bare feet,
I happen upon a large city.
Hustle was the game.
I stare into a café window.
People ignore or don't notice my gaunt appearance.
In it's reflection are the supple steps and sounds
of busy.
Everyone needs to be somewhere.
The reverberation of life is loud to me.
Soon enough,
I pass through endless alleys,
crowds,
and roads.
I find myself at a small shop,
pastries lining the front.
I walk up, smile,
and quietly take a scone.

EPILOGUE
III

Getting over it wasn't easy.
Now that I'm a bird,
I adorn new clothes.
I try to meet other people.
Being in the new world is daunting.
It's inviting,
too.
The guise of the fruit still haunts me.
Some people say nice things,
others say nothing.
I still wonder of their perception through their stark eyes.
Whether they think
I'm a fallen angel
or a picture on their mantle.

AUTHORS NOTE:

Through all of the suffering I endured
Deep down,
I knew I must keep my heart open.
So that whatever comes my way,
in new forms
or what leaves with a ceasless goodbye...
Is seen as equal footing.
The love will always be here.
I am here.

Thank you. Thank you for reading.
You are unconditionally loved.
Whether you like it or not.
;)

9 798995 899303